I Like Flowers

by

Rick Malm

I Like Flowers

First Printing 2017

Published by Orekid Books
An imprint of Ore Publishing
Texas

ISBN 978-0-9985085-0-4

Author Contact:
Richard Malm
P.O. Box 291002
Kerrville, TX 78029-1002
Rick@OrePublishing.com

Copyright © 2017 by Richard Malm
All rights reserved. This book or any portion thereof may not be reproduced or used in any manner whatsoever without the express written permission of the publisher except for the use of brief quotations in a book review.
Printed in the United States of America

OREkid Books
an imprint of Ore Publishing
Mining and Sharing Riches Through Writing

This book belongs to a wonderful child named

_____

I
like
flowers.
They smell so
Sweet.

They're nice

to look at

but ....

I watch them

Dance

with

gentle ease,

When softly touched by **Puffy Breeze.** I like flowers.

I like flowers.
I'll tell you why.
Cause hummingbirds
and butterflies
will often take
a flower STOP

I like flowers
with colors bright;
RED, YELLOW, PURPLE,

Even

White.

They're fun
to pick
and give away,

a perfect gift for *Mother's day.*

I like flowers.

I like flowers

but

please

BEWARE.

Bees like flowers.

So take great

CaRxe

When

smelling flowers,

like a

Rse,

Make sure no bee goes up your nose!

OUCH!

I

like

flowers.

I like flowers
and
pretty leaves.

Spring's blossoms look like flower trees.

Red, orange, yellow, brown, gold and green.

Autumn leaves make a pretty scene.

but

I like flowers.

I like flowers when they're alone.

I like them covering a Stone.

I like flowers mile upon mile.

A flower ocean makes me smile.

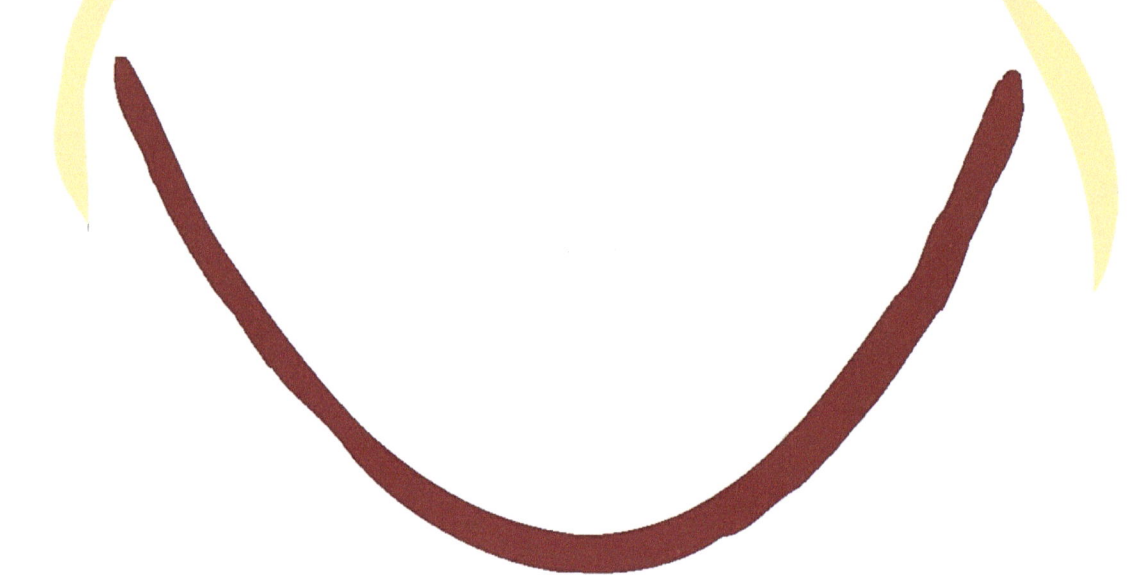

I
like flowers.

I like flowers but some seem mean.

Their sticky thorns can make me scream!

OUCH! OUCH! I yell,

"You made me cry!"

Sometimes
it makes me
wonder why

I like flowers.

Now it's
your turn
to tell me why

you like flowers
and butterflies.

Do you like little buzzy bees?
Do you like pretty Autumn leaves?

I hope you enjoyed *I Like Flowers* and that you and your child will have fun reading it together again and again.

Children are a lot like flowers. Each is a unique and fragile creation reflecting the beauty and splendor of the heavenly Father. They grow best when cared for but are easily overlooked, ignored and taken for granted. They also quickly mature and are gone. But, if raised carefully, they go to spread the color and fragrance of their lives with many others.

As you and your child share *I Like Flowers* I hope each photo will remind you of the beautiful and special treasure God has given you in your child and that you'll lavishly communicate that sense of awe and love to your child each time you read it.

I'd love to hear from you with any comments or thoughts.

Rick@orepublishing.com

www.ingramcontent.com/pod-product-compliance
Lightning Source LLC
Chambersburg PA
CBHW042008100426
42738CB00040B/100